CW01067572

MIDLAND MEMORIES

MIDLAND MEMORIES

Lucy D. Williams

ARTHUR H. STOCKWELL LTD
Torrs Park Ilfracombe Devon
Established 1898
www.ahstockwell.co.uk

British Library Cataloguing-in-Publication Data.
A catalogue record for this book is available
from the British Library.

Dedication:
To true friendship.

ISBN 978-0-7223-4071-4
Printed in Great Britain by
Arthur H. Stockwell Ltd
Torrs Park   Ilfracombe
Devon

CONTENTS

Morning Prayer 7
Winter Sunshine 8
I Believe 9
A Prayer at Dawn 10
Days Like These 11
Counting Our Blessings 12
Storm Force 13
March of Time 14
Home Town 15
To Dennis 16
Springtime Prayers 17
Day by Day 18
The Things I Know 20
Love Me 21
The Place 22
Lovely Hurst Green 23
Thank You 24
Harvest Time 25
A Wonderful World 26
Return of the Gasmen 27
Winter 28
Our Lord's Blessings 29
Pause For Thought 30
Evening Solace 32
Halesowen 33
With Humble Hearts 34
My Church 35
Watching the Birds 36
Uncle John 37
My Pal Whiskey 38
Gary 39
Mountains and Carousels 40
Considerations 41
The Table 42
Mr Frost 43
Treasures 44
Time 45
A Christmas Gift 46

On Rainy Days   47
Questions   48
Walk with Me   49
Funny Old World   50
Wild Ginger   51
Our Congregation   52
Remembering   53
Outstretched Arms   54
Vantage Point   55
The GCSE Blues   56
A Country Run   58
Mr Sun   60
The Church   61
The Song   62
Expectancy   63
The Pipes   64

MORNING PRAYER

In the early morning light, this day,
Dear Lord, please listen, as I pray.
Be with me every waking hour.
Let not my voice or face be sour.
Please show me how to be a friend
To those whose troubles never end.
If I could hold a shaking hand,
And help that person once more to stand
Straight and tall, and facing life,
Just fighting back, whatever the strife,
Then, once more, to You I'd raise
A silent prayer of thanks and praise.
And, when for me, life's getting tough,
When the doctor's pills are not enough,
Give me the strength to fight the pain,
To shake off sorrow and smile again,
For I know, dear Lord, deep in my heart,
Your love for me will never depart,
And You will be my rock, my friend,
For evermore, until life's end.

Amen.

WINTER SUNSHINE

Pale, bright, winter sunshine
Through my window streaming,
Etching bare, black branches,
Sets every snowflake gleaming.
I feel the gentle warmth
Touching my face and arm,
Lighting this little room of mine
With a warming, cheerful charm.

A gentle breeze stirs nearby trees,
A robin sings, and jenny wren,
And in the distance a collared dove
Softly coos, again and again,
As I gaze out at this winter scene,
Winter wonderland, with signs of spring,
Crocus and daffodil poking through,
Heralding what coming weeks will bring.

So once again, Our Lord above
Has helped us safely through
The ravages of winter storms.
He's shown us what to do.
So now I bow my head in prayer,
And, touched by the late winter sun,
I thank Him for the blessings and love
He's given to me, and everyone.

I BELIEVE

In this modern day and age,
When life seems fast and hard,
And nobody trusts his neighbour,
Everyone is on his guard.
All the cynics scoff out loud,
"There ain't no God, only hell for you."
Well, if you believe there is a hell,
Then you must believe in heaven too!

Life's moments run in opposites,
In their wisdom scientists say,
And I believe this fact is true,
So I'm very pleased to state today
I'd sooner have Jesus in my heart
Than all the gold that's in Fort Knox.
And, in my soul, the love of God
Means more than treasures in a box.

How can they say there is no God,
When you watch the sun rising high in the sky
Or hold your partner's hand in yours,
As you hear your baby son's first cry?
When tears of happiness cloud your eyes
As your lovely daughter vows, "I do."
So many times I truly thank Our Lord;
So many times you should thank Him too.

A PRAYER AT DAWN

Dear Lord, please hear me as I pray,
Bringing You thanks for a brand-new day,
The pinks and golds of the early dawn,
And glistening dew on a fresh-mown lawn,
For the soft perfume of the flowers of the spring,
Whose colours could rival a butterfly's wing,
Fresh green leaves on branches so high,
Fluffy white clouds in a deep-blue sky.

A gentle spring breeze that kisses me,
And stirs the young leaves on the old oak tree,
Carrying the dancing damselflies
That bob about neath the brightening skies.
I have no words to describe the love
That You give to mankind from heaven above.
I can only hope that my humble prayer
Will wing its way to join others up there.

For all mankind on this world must see
That without Your love and compassion we
Would be lost for ever. Then where would we be?
No love, and no hope for them or me.
So, thank You, dear Lord, for Your blessings and love,
That touches us all, like soft rain from above.
Be with us all now, and every day,
And guide and protect us along life's way.

Amen.

DAYS LIKE THESE

Sometimes, life, it seems such a bore!
The ironing's become a hateful chore,
And the kids are screaming – won't go to bed.
There's a great big drum pounding in your head!

When work, today, is a blinking pain,
The printout paper's jammed again!
A bad-tempered boss says your hair's a mess –
When what the customer wants is anybody's guess!

Visitors arrive – you've flour on your face,
Your souffle's fallen, flat on its face!
Hubby's home, had a real bad day,
In no mood for a kiss – or to hear what you say!

All on your own, alone in your home,
Your aching heart's with him, wherever he may roam.
Love is so longing for his touch,
Wanting to hold him, ever so much!

At times like these, now who could say
How on earth you can get through the long, long day.
But, just turn to the One who's your real, true friend,
For God will love you, and comfort you, until life's end.

Amen.

COUNTING OUR BLESSINGS

The blessings of Our Lord above
Are everywhere you look,
In an old and faded photograph
Or the pages of a book.

In the warm and dappled sunshine
Through leaves so fresh and green,
Or holding baby in your arms
When she's washed, so soft and clean.

In the trusting eyes of your old dog
With his head resting on your knee,
And children's happy laughter
When they all come round for tea.

Relaxing on a sandy beach,
Listening to the sounds of the sea,
Singing His praises in an old small church,
Or listening to a blackbird in a tree.

We were given a heart, eyes and ears
To appreciate such things –
The many blessings of Our Lord,
Our great, true King of Kings.

STORM FORCE

I woke suddenly from my dream
Head raised, listening – what's that?
Rain, myriads of glistening
Pebbles sanding the windows,
Driven by a furious force
That hummed its sinister song
In the confines of the chimney.

I glanced at the clock – 3 a.m.
'Good grief,' I thought, 'what a night!'
Insidious sounds filled my home
As the cruel wind, denied, threshed
The defenceless trees whose tortured
Shadows writhed on my bedroom
Wall – I could close eyes but not ears.

Suddenly, a splintering crash
That sent me, scrambling, towards
The window. A tree was down, smashed
Against a shattered fence. Torn,
Twisted roots pointed forlornly
Upwards as the storm-force wind
Increased to terrifying strength

Hitting the house, again, again
Shaking, buffeting, shaking
It to the very foundations –
I backed away, trembling, scared.
As I crept downstairs to brew some
Tea, I mouthed a silent prayer –
Thank God for double glazing!

MARCH OF TIME

There is an old saying, so I'm told,
That sometimes time stands still,
But time has not stood still near here,
On the sides of Rowley Hill.

For, as I've journeyed to and fro
From Dudley to Blackheath Town,
I've watched the hedges being pulled out,
And the lovely trees torn down.

Then, so the march of time began . . .
Where horses used to roam,
Spread rows and rows of boxes,
Little houses, folk call home.

And on the other side of the hill,
The quarry grows and grows,
'Controlled blasting' for granite chips.
Will it end? Well, no one knows!

But now, in pockets very small,
The wildlife clings on tight.
There, time and life are standing still
Till it's time to get up and fight!

HOME TOWN

I strolled alone, in the cool evening air,
Past Birmingham's Symphony Hall.
My mind went back to the days of my youth,
When buildings weren't nearly so tall.

Broad Street was quiet, just the odd car or two,
Not crammed with traffic, nose to tail.
Pavements weren't crowded with jostling folk,
Your ears not blasted by a police car's wail.

You could sit on a bench, enjoying warm summer sun,
In the grounds of the old Hall of Memory,
Then around 4 p.m. just a short walk
To the café for your afternoon tea.

But, that has all gone now, the peace and the quiet.
In my mind, a precious memory,
For Birmingham's grown, both upwards and out.
There's no place for an old 'un like me!

But despite all the hustle, and bustle and noise,
Birmingham's home town to me,
For I am a Brummie, born and bred,
And for all of my life so will be.

TO DENNIS

So deep, the darkness of the night,
But there a lone star twinkles bright,
And then a flit of moonlight touched a tree
Whose bare 'arms' reflect the ache in me.

Where are you now, my dearest dear?
Now I can never hold you near.
My empty arms reach out in vain,
For you will never come again.

So many years have rolled away
Since on our lovely wedding day
We promised both to love and cherish.
And love held fast; it did not perish.

Through times of joy, and times of sorrow,
We never worried about tomorrow –
Was there enough to pay the rent? –
Or wondered where our wages went!

And now I'm old, and live alone,
But never truly on my own,
For tho' death keeps us two apart
Your memory lives deep in my heart.

SPRINGTIME PRAYERS

It's the season that we all call spring.
It's the season when the buds start to grow,
When all the little birds start to sing.
It's the reason that our hearts start to glow.

So let God's love flow over like a silver stream.
Take Him into your heart, and you will know
That His love will fill your soul, and you will gleam
Like the twinkling stars, or a flake of purest snow.

Your spirits will lift, and your heart will sing.
Let those waters wash all your sins away.
Your life will be enriched, and His love will bring
A cheerful mind, to keep those blues at bay.

His love will live longer; His love is always true,
And, like this season that we all call spring,
The warmth of His love will warm us through and through.
So come and lift up your voices and sing . . .

Sing to Him praises for the blessings we receive,
And for the love that surrounds in every way.
He will guide us and protect us, and He will never leave
Us, which is why we pray and thank Him on this lovely spring day.

DAY BY DAY

When I was only five, the world seemed so alive –
That's how it always seemed to me.
Mum and Dad always there, with never a care,
And then there were candles on the Christmas tree.

When I was only eight, the world was so great,
For I had a lovely two-wheeled bike.
Mum and Dad with great big grins, so busy with the twins –
Two little girls, and oh, so much alike.

When I was only ten, there were many soldier men
Fighting hard in the Second World War.
Mum and Dad, you see, joined the ARP.
There was blackout, and sandbags round the door.

When I was eleven, many folk had gone to heaven.
There were holes where the houses used to be.
Mum and Dad often sad, things were getting really bad –
I was on a train, another frightened evacuee!

When I was fifteen, waving flags could be seen,
Celebrating the end of the war.
Two months later Mum and Dad left the home we'd always had;
We left old London Town for evermore.

When I was twenty-one, I was presented with a son
By the girl I was so proud to call my wife.
Mum and Dad and all agree that the baby looked like me,
Things felt so good – I was so pleased with all my life.

Suddenly I'm thirty-five – as a family we survive,
Tho' sometimes I wish that I was a child again.
Mum and Dad they do their best, but often need a rest,
And my kids they love to play out in the rain.

Then soon the big five-O. I'll be fifty then, you know,
How fast the busy years have gone on by,
And how I miss my Mum and Dad – the best you could have had!
Now I'm the head of the family and mustn't cry - not I!

And now, I'm eighty-eight, one foot through the Pearly Gate,
A great-granddad again, I'm pleased to say.
So I thank the Lord above for His blessings, and the love
He has given to my family, day by day.

THE THINGS I KNOW

Next month I will be eighty, you know,
And that's a well-known fact,
But when I think I'm still a chic young chick,
Well, it's my ego putting on an act!

My poor old hips, they creak and groan
As I'm hobbling along the street,
But a big smile – "I'm A-OK"
Greets all the people that I meet.

With arthritic fingers struggling
To open the blasted pickle jar,
My mind's again full of fantasies . . .
I'm seventeen – and a bright athletic star!

And I know, these days, my memory
Is not what it used to be –
But I can remember scrumping apples
When I was twelve, from our neighbour's apple tree!

Some say there isn't any God,
No such thing as Christianity . . .
But I know, deep within my heart,
Our dear Lord, He blesses me!

LOVE ME

The church fête was going so well
On that lovely bright day in spring.
They'd hired a local pop group
To stand on the stage and sing.
They strummed their 'lectric guitars,
And strutted about, like they do,
Singing their happy love songs,
But one looked real fed up and blue.

So our vicar, being a kindly man,
Walked up to them during the break.
He said, "You look so sad, lad.
You look as if your heart would break."
The young man asked the vicar,
"Please tell me where I've gone wrong."
Then sadly picking up his guitar,
He started to sing his song.

The vicar climbed on to the stage,
Looked the singer straight in the eye.
"Change the words of your life's song, son.
You can if you really try."
Just sing, "Dear Lord, please love me,
Like nobody else can do.
Change my life, and lead me –
Lead me right home to You."

THE PLACE

Quinton Cemetery's just up the road, you know,
With a bit of spare land at the side,
And if you sit quiet, in your window at night,
You can watch mother fox, full of pride.

And then there's the birds, of all colours and size,
When they come to our gardens for food,
The pigeons, feasting on fresh-sown lawn seed,
And the starlings, with their noisy young brood.

There's blackbirds, robins, and wee jenny wrens,
Little blue tits, that hunt round the flowers,
The perfume of roses, the sigh of the trees.
I could sit in my garden for hours!

I don't want to move to a city or town,
Even if they're the finest to be seen,
For this is the place, with its gardens and trees,
Our small and modest Hurst Green.

LOVELY HURST GREEN

In the heart of a city,
Tell me, what do you see?
A fragrant rose garden
Or a flowering apple tree?

In the heart of a city,
Tell me, what do you hear?
A blackbird's morning song,
Or the call of a deer?

No! For skyscrapers loom,
Reaching up to the sky,
And the air's full of fumes
From the traffic rumbling by.

So I'll keep my little home
In our lovely Hurst Green,
With its colourful gardens,
And the air, sweet and clean.

If I were offered a fortune,
I'm afraid I'd turn it down,
For I much prefer the countryside
To a noisy, bustling town.

THANK YOU

Let's raise our hands and thank Our Lord
For the summer that's just gone by.
Thank Him for the lovely flowers
And the sun up in the sky.

For the wonderful holidays we've had
In places far away,
But most of all let's thank Him for
His blessings, given every day.

Now thank Him for the golden tints
On many shades of green,
For combine harvesters and crops,
And field mice, rarely seen.

For spiders' webs, sparkling with dew,
The last rose and the acorns,
And thank Him that we're still here to see
All these lovely autumn dawns.

HARVEST TIME

When autumn comes, she will unfold
Her gown of russet red and gold,
And at this lovely time, it's true,
We gather crops in – quite a few!

To celebrate this great event,
Food of many kinds is sent
To lots of schools and churches where
We lift our voice in song and prayer.

So let us all, with one accord,
Sing our songs to praise the Lord,
And give our thanks in prayer once more
For all the food we have in store.

A WONDERFUL WORLD

As a cool spring breeze
Stirs fresh green on the trees
And a warming sun streams through the window,
I sit, warm and snug,
Hot coffee in my mug,
And watch the wild birds come and go.

As I watched with delight
This wonderful sight,
I couldn't help thinking, you know,
That our dear Lord above
Blessed us all with a love
For wild birds, from little wrens to a crow.

How gracious is He
To have given you and me
Eyes and ears to observe His creations!
So let us rejoice,
And all with one voice
Bring Him praises throughout all the nations.

RETURN OF THE GASMEN

All the neighbours in our street,
From one to sixty-five,
We thought the work was finished –
Till we saw the trucks arrive!

"Good gracious me!" the cry went up,
Well, here we go again,
We know the work's essential,
But it isn't half a pain!

Yellow pipes, both large and small,
All piled up by the score,
Purple barriers, pneumatic drills,
Holes appearing by your door.

Great big vans, parked nose to tail,
Traffic lights 'most everywhere,
Cars and folk, risking life and limb –
Cross the road now, if you dare!

But all the residents like me
Give the workmen a cheerful grin,
While saying quietly under our breath,
"Go to it lads – one day you'll win!"

WINTER

Winter is the crafty one!
He sneaks quietly behind
Autumn's skirts, scattering
Frost and ice at the feet
Of the unwary, and laughs
In the wind. He pinches
Red noses, pokes with icy
Fingers through cracks, feeling,
Seeking unprotected
Water pipes. In mellow mood
Will blanket homes and gardens
In purest white and bow
Branches of tall conifers
With weights of sparkling snow.
The earth is quiet as though
Asleep. Only the crows
With raucous cries disturbing
The peace, until the wind,
Rising, moans through stark, bare
Branches, strums telephone
Wires, then all doors and windows
Shut tight to keep winter out!

OUR LORD'S BLESSINGS

How good the Lord has been to me,
Throughout my varied life –
All through the years when I was young,
The years when I was just the wife.

But, now I'm old and on my own,
I can chuckle to myself
At some of the things I've heard folk say –
"Oh, she's well and truly on the shelf!"

On the shelf? I don't think so!
For friends, I've quite a few.
Some are old and grey like me;
To others life is fresh and new,

But the ones this old girl values most
Are the three that visit me –
Three cute and cuddly 'little folk'
Aged eight and five and three.

So to Our Lord I give my thanks
For the blessings He has shown.
With a child's trust, and friendships old,
The Lord never leaves me on my own.

PAUSE* FOR THOUGHT

It came by post, that little
Book of poems – forty-one pages,
Mostly blank verse, but some rhymed.
Blank verse or prose? Who knows?
Too deep for me, a simple soul!
I am as a little child at her
Mother's knee, learning.
And, in that learning,
Should I write the lines: "And
The black cat pounced, and tore
The robin, and licked the blood"?
I think not! It gives me
Pause for thought.

A book of poems. I read it
Through. Poetry or prose? I am
As a little child, learning. To me,
Should not a poem flow as a
Twinkling burn or springtime's
Melting snows? And should the lines
Be written so: '*I see the winding*
Water make a short and then a
Shorter lake, as here stand I,
And house-boat high survey the
Upper Thames.'† And quote.
That sounds better! It gives me
Pause for thought.

I will read, listen and try to
Learn. What is to be learned?
Blank verse! Rhyme or prose? Who
Knows! This child with library books
And cassette tapes would a poet
Make? Maybe. We will see. In time,
If she should find the words
To catch the imagination of
The minds of others, will they
Listen? A book of poems. Not
Very big. Forty-one pages, and
Reading through it gives me
Pause for thought.

* *Pause*, issued by the National Poetry Foundation.
† Taken from John Betjeman's *Collected Poems*,
'Henley-on-Thames'.

EVENING SOLACE

Evening, washed bright blackness
That enfolds me,
Taps cool fingers on my cheeks
And strokes my hair,
Fast cars hiss on glistening
Roadways – headlights
Crystallizing randy raindrops.
Those streaming specks
Of light are falling fireflies . . .

Lifting my face
To kisses of the evening,
Breathe the body
Of the night, so fresh and clean,
Soft caressing
Cascades from the night sky cools
My anger, allowing heart
And mind to breathe.

HALESOWEN

Halesowen once was a very quiet place,
Just a little village, that's for sure,
Where, on Sundays, the children would all come to church
With a well-scrubbed face – and most demure!

Miners' cots were dotted here and there,
And plenty of old pubs too.
There was lots of room in the post office where
You could chat, while you stood in the queue.

Well-run schools, and little corner shops,
A few more, as Halesowen grew.
You could walk down the lanes, past fields of crops,
Cattle and sheep, and orchards too.

But modern Halesowen isn't like that now,
For 'progress' has put a stop to that!
There are car parks and offices where you used to see a cow.
In the new post office you couldn't swing a cat!

Well, though there are traffic jams, and pavements full of people,
There's a topic now that binds us all together.
Tho' the roads are all congested, we can still observe the steeple,
While we chat amongst ourselves – about the weather!

WITH HUMBLE HEARTS

Dear Lord, we lift our praise to You,
For the sun up in the sky,
The warm but gentle summer breeze,
And the white clouds drifting by.

We praise You for the lovely songs
Of the birds, both large and small,
For the beautiful flowers, the rippling grass,
And the trees all standing tall.

We give our thanks for the many crops
All ripening in the fields:
Potatoes, carrots, peas and beans –
For *all* the bounteous yields.

Our hearts are full of wonder, Lord,
That for us You've so much love,
For we are just such little specks
In the universe above.

All through our lives, with humble hearts,
We'll give our thanks to You,
For You're our God, our faithful friend,
No matter what we do.

MY CHURCH

My church is not much to look at,
Its members just number a few,
But the warmth and love that is found there
Embraces both me and you.

When you're lost in despair, and are lonely,
If you're ill and can't get around,
As one they all pull together –
They won't let your life run aground.

So, as long as I can, I'll continue
To go to this church, although small.
It's full of God's wonderful blessings,
That fall, like a cloak, on us all.

WATCHING THE BIRDS

I see a flock of starlings cross the sky,
And wonder where they're going to, and why.
And there, a lone seagull glides on a breeze
That plucks at skirts, at brollies and at trees.

Watch the pied wagtail acting the clown,
Runs a few steps, then bobs up and down.
Then a blackbird comes. Just watch him pick
A piece of bread up, then run off so quick.

Here comes a robin, hopping down the path,
He pecks a crumb or two, then takes a bath.
Just listen to the sparrows chirp and flutter,
Frightened by the magpie's loud, brash stutter.

I wouldn't sell my cosy little home
To buy a penthouse, or a flat in Rome,
For from my 'hide', my little upstairs window,
I can watch my lovely wild birds come and go.

UNCLE JOHN

Uncle John, dear Uncle John,
You're sixty-seven today, they say,
So your friends here would like to say
To you *a very happy birthday*.

Dear Uncle John, let's have no moans
About those many birthdays gone.
Come on now – no more groans!
You're sprightly and, we think, quite handsome!

You dig the garden, paint the house,
Polish the car quite brightly,
And we think (just for your spouse)
You'd dance the hornpipe twice nightly!

May the Good Lord, in His wisdom,
Grant you birthdays, many more.
May He bless and keep you safe
And grant you happiness in store.

Come raise your mug of tea with me
And to the future drink,
To health and wealth and happiness
And hope we're always in the pink!

HAPPY 67th BIRTHDAY.

HAPPINESS IS A STATE OF MIND

MY PAL WHISKEY

In the days of the Second World War,
When things were getting so bad,
And fresh eggs, meat and poultry
Were just nowhere to be had,
My dad went down to the market
And bought twenty-four day-old chicks,
All fluffy yellow – all 'cept one,
Black and white, up to all sorts of tricks!

And I loved that cheeky young chick,
For I was a child, aged nine.
Although he was smaller than the rest,
Little Whiskey, well, he was *mine*!

But one day, just before Christmas,
Another neighbour came around,
And when I arrived home from school
Little Whiskey couldn't be found!
How I cried when I found my pal Whiskey
Was going to be somebody's dinner!
But I still have two of his feathers,
And I still think my dad was a sinner!

GARY

He was our son, our little boy,
A regular scamp, but brought such joy.
He loved his life, his girls, his plane,
But he will ne'er come home again.

We'll never know the reason why
In Scotland cold he had to die.
At only forty-six years old
He'd half his life still to unfold.

Tho' coming years they will not tarry,
He'll always be our lovely Gary.
In memory and many a heart
He'll always be a precious part.

MOUNTAINS AND CAROUSELS

I have lived a long and eventful
Life. Now I am old, aged eighty-seven.
I stand at the foot of this mountain
Slope called stairs, and wait
For the hammer of my heart to subside.

With steps as weary as my heart
And mind, I climb these stairs
That seem steeper every year, to ride
Again the night-time carousel
Of darkness, loneliness and fear.

The sunset fades, and night-time creeps
Into my room, a dark and an unwelcome
Ghost. Cold insidious fingers of fear
Stir the nameless horrors that hide
In the dark recesses of my mind.

A mountain climbed, a heart that thumps
Its warning message in my chest. Yet,
Blind stubbornness denies the safety
Of a bed downstairs. So I will climb
My mountain, and ride my carousel till death
Puts on the brakes, and I can rest.

CONSIDERATIONS

Consider the home help:
A better name than 'cleaner'
Don't you think?

What are her duties?
She shops and cleans, cooks
Nutritional values.

One of her talents:
When to be heard, when *not*
To be seen.

Consider her feelings:
Sometimes loved, sometimes
Looked down on.

Feel her emotions
When friendships formed are
Lost in death.

What is she worth?
Banned by the union
From striking.

Consider the home help:
Value for money.

THE TABLE

Away and away, my thoughts fly away,
Listening to the surf's soft boom,
To a tiny garden far away
Where there isn't very much room

For the lilac tree, the apple tree,
The fir trees, all a-sighin'
Round a tiny lawn. My! The size of a pea,
Where Granny sat, a-cryin'.

"What are you cryin' for, Granny?" I said.
"Why, the poor little robin is dead, is dead,
All cos he liked a bit of bread,"
Said Granny, cryin'.

"Well, cats there are many, 'tis true, 'tis true.
'Twas a black one that crouched in flowers so blue,
Waiting for robin as down he flew . . .
And cats will do what cats will do."

"Now cheer up, Granny," I quickly replied.
"I'll build you a table
Where cats are not able
To pounce on the birds, tho' they hide."

In the cold light of dawn
By a very small lawn
Stands a table strong and tall,
Where little birds feed on bread, nuts and seed,
Safe from the cats, where they crawl.

On a cool summer night, with the stars shining bright,
And the breeze through the palm trees sighin',
I remember that lawn, in the cold light of dawn,
And my granny smilin', not cryin'.

MR FROST

I do not like you, old Jack Frost.
A lot of money you have cost us,
Slipping icy fingers round our pipes!
Your frosty breath with glee you blows
Round my ribs and up my nose,
And on the windows a lacy pattern types!

All through the winter you have fun
On starry nights, days bright with sun,
Or like today, when it is dull and cloudy.
Still, never mind, it won't be long
Before the birds, throats full of song,
Will greet the dawn; and Spring,
She will say, "Howdy!"

TREASURES

Honeysuckle, humming bees,
Summer breeze and almond trees,
Sweet alyssum, sage in flower,
Fresh-mown grass and currants (sour),
Garden mint and rosemary,
Chives and lettuce for my tea,
Ladybirds and butterflies,
Caterpillars, clear blue skies,
Bright geraniums on fire,
Sweet peas climbing up the wire,
Cabbages and potatoes,
Spinach, parsnips in straight rows,
Apple trees and bird table,
Cooing doves high on the gable.

God gives these gifts to all who toil
To plant the seed and till the soil,
So never mind the aching back,
Arthritic hips and hands that crack,
For our dear Lord provides us all
With food to eat, and leaves that fall.
Bright scented flowers, graceful trees –
He fills our lives with such as these,
And so with grateful hearts we raise
Hands and voice with songs of praise,
To thank our dear Lord once again
For all He gives, yes, even rain!

TIME

After days have lurched into weeks,
And the weeks have slid into months,
My strangling, searing, pain of concern
Lies dormant, quiet volcano. . . .

He sleeps softly, my man, my love,
Pale hands on the sheet, quiet now,
Thin face just touched with the palest rose –
A hint of returning health.

Time to sit on the side of his bed,
Time to notice the world passing by,
To wish for the skills of an artist –
Paint the wonderful sunsets I've watched.

Time to think of the weeks that have passed,
Of the constant support we've received,
To thank God for the most precious gift –
The life of the man that I love.

A CHRISTMAS GIFT

The bustle of the day has ceased
And all is quiet and still.
Soon, little stars come twinkling out
While the moon rides o'er the hill.
And all our little children
Are tucked up safe in bed,
Unlike Mary, Mother of Our Lord,
Who had nowhere to lay her head.

The tired children sleep and dream
Of the wonderful day to come,
With presents under the Christmas tree
And *the cake* – made by their mum!
Then, as we give our Christmas presents
To our loved ones, near or afar,
Just remember the Three Wise Men of old
Who followed a bright new star.

Then by a manger were gently laid
Myrrh, frankincense and gold –
Gifts humbly given by three kings,
A true story, now so old.
So, as you celebrate today,
Keep God's gift within your heart,
Lord baby Jesus, born to die,
To give us a brand-new start.

ON RAINY DAYS

When the day is so grey
And full of cold rain,
When going to work
Is such a big pain,
The cat looks bedraggled,
The garden is soaked –
Well, believe it or not,
The car has just croaked!

But we won't be downhearted, will we?
No, we'll wait for the warm days of spring,
And all come to church with a glad heart.
We'll raise up our voices and sing –
Sing praises and prayers to our dear Lord,
For He knows that we have to have rain
And He knows just when is the right time
To send out the sunshine again.

Then when work is done
And we're home once again,
Who cares about cold winds,
The sleet and the rain?
As we sit by the fire
With a nice cup of tea
We can say with a sure heart,
"I have someone who loves me."

QUESTIONS

Were there daffodils in flower
When they crucified Our Lord?
Did catkins and pussy willows
Shed golden tears abroad?

And when the skies grew dark
O'er that stark and lonely hill,
Did life go on the same way,
Or did everything stand still?

And were His anguished cries of pain
Echoed by the wild birds?
And did a soft and gentle breeze
Carry His dying words?

"Father, forgive them," were the words that He said,
"For they know not what they do."
Was ever such a wonderful love shown
For mankind, the whole world through!

WALK WITH ME

When winter's keen and icy winds
Still seek out water pipes (at cost!)
And we are feeling so fed up
For sunshine seems completely lost.

Then take my hand, dear Lord above.
Walk through this world with me,
And give me strength and courage
Until better times I see.

Just let me see the signs of spring:
A snowdrop peeping through,
Catkins shaking in the breeze,
An early crocus, one or two.

If You will take my hand, dear Lord,
Walk through this world with me,
Then I can face the future,
Stand strong, like a tall oak tree.

And as days start to lengthen,
And tomorrow has a brighter hue,
Then I am truly thankful, Lord,
That I walked this world with You.

FUNNY OLD WORLD

It's a funny old world that we live in,
And some folk are funnier too!
Take the strapping young chap in his new suit
Bemoaning the fact that it's blue!
Or the well-upholstered old lady
Flashing her large diamond ring –
She says the increase in her pension
Won't pay for a cruise, poor old thing!

You could go on for ever and ever,
If you sat down and thought it all through,
About the very large contrasts
Between people's lives, and it's true.
For we tend to forget, in our hurry,
How really well off we all are
Compared to the lives of so many
In other lands, both near and afar.

But the one thing we all have in common
Is the love of our dear Lord above,
For whatever life brings along the way
He blesses us all with His love.
So come on, my friends, and raise your hands,
And sing as loud as you can
To thank our Saviour for all His love,
And the blessings that touch every man.

WILD GINGER

A ginger cat on my garden wall,
So lean and mean, not very tall,
With hungry eyes at me you stare
And I must come to you out there,
My food to share.

A ginger cat, with dish well licked,
So lean and mean, his thin tail flicked,
And soft the meow, and friendship grew
To last a whole long lifetime through,
Between us two.

My ginger cat with eyes of gold,
So lean and mean, is growing old,
With rasping tongue and purring song
His silky fur rubbed round my shoe.
I love you too.

No ginger cat on my garden wall,
So lean and mean and not very tall!
Now death's soft arm shields you from harm,
And I am bound by memory –
But you are free.

OUR CONGREGATION

As we gather in this ancient church,
Our tiny congregation,
We've come to seek and praise Our Lord,
Sit quiet in meditation.

And as we pray and sing our songs
The presence of Our Lord
Touches each and every one
With a familiar chord.

We feel the love that blesses all,
That binds us all together,
Giving strength to everyone,
Through hard times or bad weather.

And all our congregation,
Both the young and old,
Take to heart the stories
From the Bible that are told.

We feel the love that strengthens us,
Lifting every heart,
And we are filled with happiness
As homewards we depart.

REMEMBERING

So many things are written
About the joys of spring,
Of all the trees that blossom
And the many birds that sing.
But what about the other side
Of this familiar notion,
About the many other lands
On the far side of the ocean?

Some are dry and arid
Where it hardly ever rains
And some are just the other way
With vast and flooded plains.
Many people in the world
Don't have enough to eat;
For others just clean water
Is a very welcome treat.

How fortunate we are
In this green and fertile land,
For all our basic needs
Are found quite close to hand.
Remembering those in ravaged lands
We should thank Our Lord on high
For there but for the grace of God
Go both you and I.

OUTSTRETCHED ARMS

For so long now I've wandered
All together, yet so alone.
It's taken me years to realize
I cannot make it on my own.

But in the shelter of Your arms, Lord,
I've found the place I want to be,
Where Your love and understanding
Brings such peace and love to me.

With Your arms outstretched You guide me
As along life's path I roam,
But it's very good to know, Lord,
In the shelter of Your arms is home.

And now so quietly, when alone
My fervent prayers I bring to You
That with Your loving arms outstretched
You shelter all my loved ones too.

And tho' the world's so full of strife,
Stones and boulders on our way,
With outstretched arms You give to all
Peace, love and comfort every day.

THE GCSE BLUES

We sit on chairs of trepidation
As naughty children waiting
To be flayed with ropes of words
For all our inattentions.

We twiddle with our sharpened pencils
And writhe on padded seats.
Shoes and boots make scuffing noises
On the classroom floor.

Will it be poetry again? I wonder.
Ye gods! The very thought
Turns brave hearts to quivering jelly
And the grey matter boggles!

The perpetrator of our torment
Enters, and all are quiet,
Except a few in youthful innocence
Ignore the teacher's stare.

In our groups, we bravely battle
Essays, poetry and prose
With tutor's patience shepherding
Towards the GCSE exams.

VANTAGE POINT

The traffic snakes down Mucklows Hill,
Sends swirls of dust up grassy banks
Where dandelion and daffodil
Defy pollution's hand.

Then through Halesowen's milling crowds,
And on towards the soft Clent Hills,
We park neath gently drifting clouds
That frame the evening moon.

We find a vantage point and park,
Then from the comfort of our car
We'll watch the sunset turn to dark
Bejewelled with brilliant stars.

The necklaces of moving cars
That drift like fireflies round the hills
Are rivalling the evening stars
With their blazing headlights.

We feel the blossom-scented breeze,
And watch the distant moving lights,
While, all around, the rustling trees
Say thank You to Our Lord.

And, parked on gently sloping ground,
Neath twinkling stars and cool night air,
The blessings of Our Lord abound.
We feel them everywhere. . . .

And in the valleys down below,
From 'Kiddi' to the Rowley Hills,
The street lamps and the houses glow
With twinkling golden light.

In olden days, did horse and trap
Pause for a while on this same spot?
Did she then smile, he doff his cap
At the Clent Hills' view of 'fairyland'?

A COUNTRY RUN

The road stretched way out before us,
Bright in the glare of the sun,
Hugging the steep Welsh hillside –
A curling snake circling its prey.
In the distance are sheep on the mountain,
Bits of fluff on a green-grey rug,
Their movements barely perceptible
Like headlice on a green coat collar.

The gradient gradually steepens,
The car hums with effortless ease,
Purring as though it is happy
To be driven on a long country run.
One signpost points to the mountains,
The other one says 'Builth Wells',
Further on a sign says 'Antique Fair'.
Curious, we pulled to the side.

We paid our 50p entrance
And followed the path round the trees,
Then stopped in utter amazement
At the scene set out before us.
There were stalls of every description,
Countless items laid out on the grass,
Remnants of bygone generations
On show for the whole world to see.

Old wooden casks, wicker baskets,
Brass ornaments, old pewter mugs,
Boxes of junk, an old waggon wheel,
Old clocks, old crocks, old farm implements!
The excited cries of the children:
"Come on, Dad", "What's that, Nan?", "Over here!"
And the plaintive wail of one little girl –
"Oh, Mummy, I *do* want a wee-wee!"

We stood on the hill munching burgers,
Watching the crowds mill about.
Right at the back a grandfather clock
Moved slowly as tho' on its own.
For two hours we wandered around,
Enthralled, glimpsing into the past.
The sun blistered down. I'd love an ice cream
And my legs are beginning to ache!

We made our way back to the car
Quite pleased with what we had bought:
A pair of tatty old ink bottles
And a delicate old porcelain jug.
The blaze of a glorious sunset,
The sigh of the car passing trees,
Husband's strong hands on the steering wheel –
Contented, I nod into sleep.

MR SUN

Now, here's something to look forward to,
For summertime is here again,
Holidays and barbecues . . .
What do we get? More rain, rain, rain!

And now it's almost autumn time
No more holidays – back to school –
And still old sun, he won't come out,
The awkward, blinkin' stubborn mule!

I wouldn't hide my face away
If I were up there, Mr Sun.
I'd battle with those dark, black clouds
And smile again on everyone.

But, people, raise your eyes and look
At the wonders of the autumn:
Ripening grain, and golden leaves,
Bright colours of the chrysanthemum.

And though we moan and grumble,
Our dear Lord holds the reins,
And always provides a sunny side
To the dark clouds when it rains.

THE CHURCH

It isn't much to look at,
This little church of ours.
There's no imposing steeple,
Or beds of fragrant flowers,

But within our church's wooden walls,
All painted cream and brown,
There is another powerful Church
You won't see in any town.

It is the real Church of Our Lord,
That lives in every-heart,
A heart that beats so strong and true,
With a love that will never depart.

And the doorway into Our Lord's real Church
Is open to everyone,
Be they as poor as little church mice,
Or their gold chains weigh a ton!

Some say this country's finished,
Great Britain's missed the boat!
You'd go and jump right off a cliff
If you took notice of all they wrote!

But when we come to our little church
To pray, and give Him our praise,
No matter what the world throws at us,
We are safe in His Church, all our days.

THE SONG

In the small hours of the morning,
Before the dawn is nigh,
In the darkness of the early night,
When daylight has left the sky,

Mr Blackbird sings his lovely song
Proclaiming for all to hear
That your garden is his little world.
To his rivals he shows no fear.

Just as, for us, for everyone,
No matter where we roam,
The whole wide world for all mankind,
Is the place that we call home.

And the One who reigns over all our world,
Who guards us night and day,
Is our dear Lord, with arms outstretched,
Who will hear us when we pray.

And, like Mr Blackbird in full song,
Gives hope and courage to all who hear,
That we in peace can live each day,
Knowing our Saviour is always near.

EXPECTANCY

Christmas Day is on its way,
It'll very soon be here,
But I've been poorly for a month
And today I still feel queer!
The family called to see me,
Gave me lots of love and hugs,
But I feel that they would love to say,
"Gran, we don't want your bugs!"

They wagged their fingers at me,
Told me that I must be good.
"Now don't go doing anything silly."
I mean really, as if I would!
But I could see the expectancy
In the little children's faces,
For they knew I had to help Santa Claus
Wrap the toys and books and braces.

They told me that poor old Santa Claus
Needed lots of grandmas like me
To help him wrap up all the presents
That he leaves under every Christmas tree.
I know I'm old and live alone,
But I thank our dear Lord above
That I have such a wonderful family
At Christmas time to love.

THE PIPES

By the courtesy of our great British Gas,
They are laying new gas pipes, you know –
Miles and miles of bright yellow pipes,
Deep in the dark earth below.
Trenches are running to the right and the left,
Each with its own purple barrier.
Now there isn't much room for the family car,
Or the council's refuse carrier!

On and on the disturbance goes on,
From one end of Hurst Green to the other,
Diggers and lorries, workers and rubble,
Causing us all sorts of bother!
They dig up our gardens, pathways and pavements,
For the good of us all, so they say,
But I, like most of the neighbours round here,
Wish they'd hurry up and go away!

But the days are long gone when we chopped stick and coal,
For the fire in the old black-lead grate,
And the new pipes will bring lots more natural gas –
Better heating, better cooking – I can't wait!
So, everyone, come and join with us.
Give our thanks with prayers and singing;
Praise the Lord for all the good things
Like the pipes that this modern age is bringing.